To the golden bamboo lemur
And to Audra, my blue-eyed lemur

Copyright © 1998 Joyce A. Powzyk

Published by the National Geographic Society
1145 17th St. N.W.
Washington, D.C. 20036

Library of Congress Cataloging-in-Publication Data
Powzyk, Joyce A.
In search of lemurs : my days and nights in a Madagascar rain
forest / by Joyce A. Powzyk.
p. cm.
ISBN 0–7922–7072–X
1. Lemurs—Madagascar—Ranomafana National Park. 2. Ranomafana
National Park (Madagascar)   I. Title.
QL737.P95P69 1998
599.8'3—dc21   97-5722

The Society is supported through membership dues and income
from the sale of its educational products. Call 1-800-NGS-LINE for more information,
or visit our Web site: www.nationalgeographic.com
Printed in U.S.A.

In Search of Lemurs:

My Days and Nights in a Madagascar Rain Forest

by Joyce A. Powzyk

NATIONAL GEOGRAPHIC SOCIETY

Washington, D.C.

ACKNOWLEDGMENTS

I wish to acknowledge the following people who generously shared their research with me so I could write this book:

Patrick Daniels (Milne-Edwards' sifaka and golden bamboo lemur)
Carl Erickson, Ph.D. (aye-aye)
Paul Ferraro (Malagasy village)
David Haring (red-bellied lemur)
Claire Hemingway, Ph.D. (Milne-Edwards' sifaka)
Mary Maas, Ph.D. and Alison Jolly, Ph.D. (island history)
David Meyers, Ph.D. (golden bamboo lemur)
Deborah Overdorff, Ph.D. (red-fronted lemur and red-bellied lemur)
Jim Ryan, Ph.D. (sucker-footed bat and red forest rat)
Eleanor Sterling, Ph.D. (aye-aye)
Frances White, Ph.D. (black-and-white ruffed lemur)
Patricia Wright, Ph.D. (Milne-Edwards' sifaka and golden bamboo lemur)
Steve Zack, Ph.D. (birds).

A special thanks to the guides in Ranomafana National Park: George, Emile, Loret, William, Pierre, Richard, and Talata. Benjamin Andrianamihaja, Bengy, Lalaina, and Noely at the park office were willing to assist at any time. Special appreciation to Dr. Patricia Wright, Stephen H. Devoto, and the late Margo Marsh who made it all possible.

The National Geographic Society would also like to thank William R. Konstant, Special Projects Director, Conservation International, and co-author of Conservation International's *Tropical Field Guide Series: Lemurs of Madagascar* for his assistance, and Carl Mehler, Senior Map Editor, National Geographic Society and Jehan Aziz for map production.

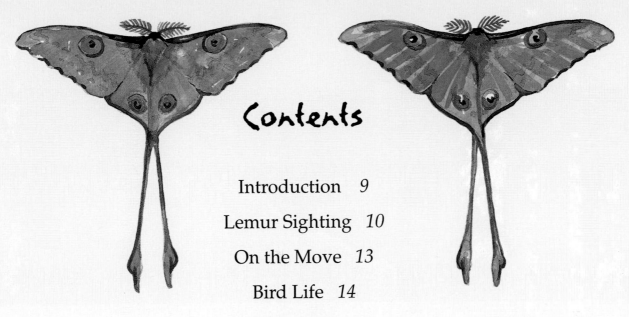

Contents

TROPIC OF CANCER

EQUATOR

TROPIC OF CAPRICORN

AFRICA

MADAGASCAR

Mozambique Channel

MADAGASCAR

Antananarivo ✪

Ranomafana
National
Park ◼

INDIAN

OCEAN

TROPIC OF CAPRICORN

Savanna

Spiny Desert

Dry Deciduous Forest

Humid Secondary Forest

Low and Mid-altitude Rain Forest

Montane, or High-altitude, Rain Forest

0   100 Miles

0   200 Kilometers

Introduction

I WANTED TO BE A BIOLOGIST EVER SINCE I WAS A LITTLE girl, searching the woods for animals near my family's home in the Adirondack Mountains of upstate New York.

While working toward a Ph.D. in animal behavior, I lived in a different forest—a lush, green, mountain rain forest in Madagascar. I was searching for lemurs.

Madagascar is the only place where all known species of lemurs can be found in the wild today, although at one time their ancestors lived throughout most of the world. In some areas they were unable to compete with their clever, large-brained relatives: the monkeys and the apes.

It is a mystery how lemurs came to live on Madagascar more than 40 million years ago. Some scientists think they may have traveled here by clinging to ocean debris or by island-hopping whenever the sea level dropped. Madagascar's environment was favorable to the lemurs, and they thrived.

I camped in Ranomafana National Park and worked with the assistance of a Malagasy guide, Talata. He is an excellent forester and animal tracker. Without his help, I never would have seen many of the animals that live in the rain forest. Lemurs ignore the biologists who work in the research area of the park because we have never harmed them. I could get close, take notes on their behavior, and make sketches of their antics.

Lemurs can be as tiny as mice or as big as dogs. They live in both dry and wet habitats. There are 32 known species of lemurs on the island. Eleven species are found in Ranomafana National Park, where it rains most days of the year. We will encounter eight of them.

Lemurs live in the forests of the world's fourth largest island. Scientists believe Madagascar separated from Africa about 150 million years ago and drifted east.

Lemur Sighting

IT'S A COLD MORNING. WE ARE WALKING THROUGH THE mud, scanning the trees for any signs of life. Suddenly Talata points to a dark shape in the tree branches. I focus my binoculars and find a furry lemur body, curled up in the V of a branch about 30 feet up from the ground.

Not meaning to, we rustle some leaves underfoot, and the lemur pops her head up and stares at us. Her eyes are large and round. Their deep amber color stands out against the black skin of her face. The daylight forces the lemur to blink as she sleepily scans the near-by trees for whatever caused the rustling sound.

We have found a rare lemur species—the Milne-Edwards' sifaka (SHE-fock)! I look around, and my excitement grows. Three other sifakas are asleep in a large harongana (har-ONG-gana) tree. This tight mass of black-and-white fur is probably two males and another female.

Even though I'm wearing long underwear, a wool sweater, and a raincoat, I'm shivering—but I don't care. I want to observe these lemurs. I want to see them move.

After licking her long arm and tapered fingers, the sifaka starts cleaning the fur on her stomach. Suddenly I see a tiny baby squirming around on her lap. Judging by its size, the baby is just a few weeks old. It looks so small and fragile—almost like a toy with a tightly curled tail.

From the other sifakas comes a low humming growl, *mmm...mmm,* a signal that the animals will soon depart from their sleep site.

The mother nuzzles her baby toward her stomach and hops along the branch. The infant instinctively grips her fur, holding on tight. A fall would mean death. An older baby nearby is strong enough to ride on its mother's back.

Its mother focuses on where she wants to go and leaps. Her arms are extended while her body is propelled by the push of powerful legs. In midair her hind legs swing forward and cushion her landing as she grabs onto a tree trunk. What an incredible way to move through the forest! Sifakas make it look easy. Because they keep their backs in an upright position when they jump, they are known as vertical clingers and leapers.

On the Move

ALL THE LEMURS ARE MOVING NOW. A MALE LANDS just beneath the mother on the same tree trunk. Because he is too close for her liking, she bends down and gives him a quick cuff on the head with her hand. He squeals in protest, but he backs down the tree, giving her lots of room. In sifaka society, as in many other lemur societies, the females dominate the males.

Talata and I follow the group of four adults into a valley between two mountain ridges. They move through the upper canopy, trees that are more than 70 feet in height. Balanced like acrobats, the sifakas feed on the young leaves and pink trumpet-shaped flowers of the tongolahy (tong-go-LA-hee), a plant related to mistletoe. This unusual plant has no roots in the ground. It is an epiphyte (eh-puh-FITE)—a plant that gets its nutrients from the air and rain. It lives high in the tree branches.

A male sifaka backs cautiously down a tree trunk, moving his arms and legs alternately to maintain his grip. He looks around for signs of danger. Everything appears safe, so he steps to the ground. For a moment the lemur stands upright on his two hind legs, just like an awkward little person.

After a few hops, the sifaka crouches and smells an exposed area of red earth. He takes a bite, hesitantly, and then takes another. Scientists don't yet understand why lemurs eat dirt. Perhaps the soil has clay particles that aid digestion or minerals that are important nutrients.

The forest is very quiet as the lemurs continue to feed. We sit on the damp forest floor, watching the group for many hours. I take careful notes on their activities in my data book, and Talata always keeps an eye on the lemurs, who are known to make fast getaways.

Bird Life

Velvet asity

SUDDENLY WE HEAR A JUMBLED NOISE LIKE THE sound of musicians warming up on their instruments. It's a mixed species flock. More than ten species of birds are moving together as a group, searching for food. By jostling the vegetation, one bird may expose insects or fruit for another bird. Traveling together brings other advantages. There are predators in the forest, and a flock has many more eyes looking for danger.

One of the first to appear is the striking blue vanga. The vanga probes the uppermost branches for insects. Exploring the middle portion of the canopy are several white-headed vangas and Pollen's vangas. The paradise flycatcher, with its long, trailing tail feathers, also stays in the middle canopy. It is an agile bird that can nab flying insects in midair. Long bristles surrounding its bill enable it to sense when food is within reach. Between meals, the flycatcher breaks into song, and its loud whistle and warble mingles with the chattering of the other birds. Low in the branches are a pair of yellow-browed oxylabes (ox-ee-LAY-bees). These small birds are searching for insects close to the ground. Toward the rear of the flock, the velvet asity scours the bushes for berries the others have missed.

Blue vanga

White-headed vanga

Different bird species occupy different levels in the forest. Some species are up high in the canopy; others are down low in the undergrowth.

The flock departs as quickly as it came, its noisy chattering fading away. There are so many things to see in a rain forest that you can lose all sense of time. We realize it's about 2:00 p.m. The day is warming, and the air now feels hot and sticky.

I peel off a layer of clothing to accommodate the change in temperature. Talata says it is cold, although I estimate the temperature to be about 75°F. But then again, he grew up here in the tropics, while I grew up with the cold, snowy winters of upstate New York.

Paradise flycatcher

Yellow-browed oxylabe

A Long Hike

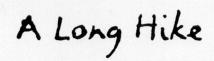

WE WALK FOR SEVERAL HOURS WITHOUT SEEING any animals. Tropical forests provide many hiding places, and although some days we are lucky enough to see wildlife, other days we see very little. But there is always the magnificent vegetation to behold. Climbing vines wrap their tendrils around a host plant and create knots of foliage. Each species of tree has a different leaf shape. Talata tells me all about the plants. He shows me a tree with bark that smells just like black licorice. He also points out a plant with stinging thorns and a vine with white, sticky sap that can cause blindness.

As the sun goes down, the green foliage loses its bright sheen. There's a faint rustling on the forest floor. In the fading light we see a greater hedgehog tenrec searching for worms, insects, and fallen fruit with its inquisitive nose. Hundreds of black-and-white spines bristle over its body as it wobbles along. These primitive tenrecs have remained unchanged for millions of years. As I try to follow it with my flashlight, the tenrec begins to feel threatened and rolls up into a tight ball, protecting its soft belly and snout with its spines. We leave it alone.

Talata and I continue along the footpath back to camp as the crescent moon rises. Small insect-eating bats zoom by our heads. But there is a larger bat here in Ranomafana—the sucker-footed bat. Another biologist is studying this species and has found that the bat spends the daylight hours in the leaf folds of a ravenala (rav-in-ALA) plant, or traveler's palm (so named because a thirsty traveler can cut into one with a machete and receive a gush of refreshing liquid). The sucker-footed bat uses the suckers on its ankles and wrists to adhere to the plant's smooth leaves, a surface too slippery for other animals.

Home Sweet Home

IT'S LATE MORNING AND WE'RE STILL AT BASE CAMP, our home away from home. I'm sitting around the roaring camp fire as Talata sifts through the rice looking for tiny rocks. This is our daily ritual, sifting rice and boiling white beans for our meals. Hot vanilla tea warms our weary bones.

The camp consists of our two dome-shaped tents and a smaller supply tent, a cook area, and a latrine—or, rather, a hole dug in the ground for a toilet. Equipment and food supplies are stored in metal trunks because everything must be kept safe from the city rats that regularly invade us. They arrived on boats along with the first human settlers and quickly spread all over the island. It's so odd to be surrounded by unusual wildlife while protecting our food against an animal that is found in garbage dumps all around the world!

Night Jumpers

AFTER OUR LATE BREAKFAST, TALATA GOES OFF TO explore a remote section of the park while cutting new trails. I venture out alone, following a trail up a mountain slope. Giant, 15-foot-tall tree ferns tower around me. Some of these ferns are more than 100 years old.

Looking up at their feathery fronds, I walk directly into the web of an orb-weaver spider. The web is incredibly strong and sticky. It takes several minutes to pull it out of my hair and off my clothes.

Up ahead, a ring-tailed mongoose is walking along the trail. Its long, weasel-like body turns and twists as it investigates every nook and cranny for a meal.

When I finally reach the upper ridge of the mountain, it's getting dark. I scan the trees with my flashlight, searching for lemurs by looking for the bright reflection in their eyes—the eyeshine—from the flashlight.

Talata told me this was a favorite area for the avahi (a-VAH-hee) lemurs to sleep during the day. They are nocturnal, or active at night. Remarkably, they are just where he said they would be, in a thicket at the trail marker for 3,000 feet. (Most trails are labeled with flags every 30 feet so no one will get lost.)

There are two avahi huddled together. It's pitch-black now, and they are waking up. The glow from their eyes is an intense orange, like the embers from my cook fire. I envy their silky fur, which looks warm on this chilly night.

One avahi leaps from its perch. I wish I could see as well in the dark as this animal can. The avahi's oversize eyes take in the light from the stars and the moon, giving it excellent night vision.

The other avahi readies itself for departure and then springs, using strong hind legs to catapult itself into the air. The pair bound through the forest, moving from one tree trunk to another like they're on pogo sticks. They are vertical clingers and leapers like the sifakas.

As I struggle to keep my light beam on their movements, I notice the white stripes that run down each of their back legs. Perhaps these leg stripes allow avahi to keep track of each other's movements in the dark forest. The two animals pause on the same tree trunk, one above the other. I sketch one carefully. Its leg is bent up against its chest, its arms wrapped tight around the tree. Avahi are monogamous, taking only one mate at a time. In contrast, sifakas have one or two mates.

The pair quietly rests and begins to nibble on the young leaves and bark of the canarium (ka-NAIR-ree-um) tree. The male sounds a short *tuif* call, a reassuring contact call that all is well. But close by I hear an animal moving along the ground. In the darkness I can't make out what it is. Suddenly the avahi are frightened and emit a series of piercing *a-vah-HEEE* calls in alarm. I now know where they get their name! They flee through the trees for safer feeding grounds. I can't follow them; there are no trails in that part of the forest.

What scared them? Whatever it was, it was too dark for me to see.

The Company of a Mouse Lemur

IT'S DIFFICULT TO GET OUT OF MY COZY SLEEPING BAG today. All my belongings are damp and moldy, and I have too many bug bites. I want to just keep sleeping—but I can't! Something that I've never seen before may be just outside my tent.

The morning sky is menacingly dark. Gray clouds continue to move in from the east. Promising myself a bath—when it's sunny—I pull on my dirty clothes and rain gear.

The patter of rain begins slowly and quickly develops into a torrent. The vegetation bends under its force. Every leaf is dripping as Talata and I eat breakfast and set out, bowing our heads to the rain.

After some distance Talata pauses to pick up a small rufous mouse lemur that is lying helpless on the ground. What happened here? Perhaps the little lemur was foraging for insects during the night and was attacked by a Madagascar great horned owl. The tiny creature is still alive but its eyes are shut, and it is barely breathing. Only six inches long, the rufous mouse lemur is one of the world's smallest living primates. As a scientist, I know that it is best not to interfere, yet I tuck the tiny animal under my shirt, against my skin, in an attempt to keep it warm.

As we walk, I keep checking on my little companion, whose fur feels soft against my belly. We come to an unusual area of the forest where thick grass grows underfoot. Looking up, I see big gaps in the leafy canopy. Here the sun can penetrate, and a soft carpet of grass is able to grow.

A red forest rat emerges from one of the many passageways through the thick ground cover. This animal is a deep burnt-orange color, and each hair is tipped with black. Its fur is wet and matted, but the rain does not slow it down. In fact, this animal is more active when it rains because the rain causes fruit to fall to the ground.

When the rat stops running, I can see its sides heaving with each breath. Its nose and whiskers twitch as it sniffs the air and catches a whiff of ripening guava.

After a quick inspection, the rat bites into the soft fruit with its protruding front teeth, or incisors, and quickly eats it all.

Back at camp in the safety of my tent, I gently remove the mouse lemur from its resting place in my clothing. It looks just like a little mouse at first glance, but I keep reminding myself that it's not a rodent, it's a primate. Its brain is much larger than a mouse's brain, and it has forward-facing eyes and thumbs that can move independently. I mash up some ripe banana, and the mouse lemur manages to eat a few bites. Its eyes open and close. I hold it in my hand and marvel at its little fingers and soft fur. Before going to sleep, I wrap the lemur up in a towel and place it in a box near my cot. Unfortunately, it doesn't survive the night.

The next morning, burying the tiny creature near my tent, I feel privileged to have seen such a remarkable animal up close.

Looking for Lemur Hunters

I STAY IN MY TENT ALL DAY, RESTING AND WRITING my observations in data notebooks and in a personal journal. The occasional patter of rain on my tent breaks the silence, and I hope it doesn't continue. Tonight Talata and I are going out to observe nocturnal animals.

We set off at dusk and soon enter a darkened valley. With my headlamp on I can see the trail more clearly. After hiking about a mile in the soft rain, we sit on the forest floor to eat. I pull several cans of corned beef from my backpack and use my Swiss army knife to pry up the lids. This is our dinner—cold corned beef.

The rain finally stops and the clouds break apart, revealing the twinkling stars of the Milky Way. Talata points in the direction of an old tree stump. We have a visitor.

A fanaloka (fan-a-LOW-ka), or Malagasy striped civet (SIH-vut), emerges from the underbrush hunting for a meal or possibly following the aroma of corned beef. It stands just six feet away, its wet nose sniffing the night air. This small carnivore is only one foot tall and looks like a cat with a long face. Its light brown fur is heavily adorned with black spots, and its tail is thick.

I remember reading that fanalokas can store fat in their tails. Their bodies absorb the fat when food is scarce.

Like other animals in the park, this carnivore is accustomed to the smell and presence of people. It circles Talata and me, sniffing the ground, but we will not share our dinner. The fanaloka moves away, along the stream bank. We hear no footsteps, only the low gurgling sound of water.

This carnivore is an opportunist, hunting whatever it happens upon as it patrols the forest floor. We watch from a safe distance as it carefully wades into the stream. A ripple on the water's surface catches the fanaloka's attention. It pounces, pinning a large freshwater crab between its jaws. Leaping gingerly onto a rock, the fanaloka hesitantly releases its catch. The crab is limp. The carnivore's large canine teeth have pierced its shell, killing it. The fanaloka chews and swallows the crab's body, discarding the surrounding six legs and two pinchers. Still hungry, the fanaloka jumps back onto the stream bank and is about to search for more food when it freezes, stock-still. Its nose is in the air, sniffing deeply. Then the small carnivore flees through the undergrowth. I am puzzled. Why leave this rich hunting ground so abruptly?

The night is tranquil once again, and my ears fill with the murmuring of running water and the *errp* of tiny tree frogs. Yet it soon becomes obvious why the fanaloka fled.

The Fossa

NEAR THE RIVER'S EDGE A FOSSA (FOO-SA) APPEARS. This is the largest carnivore on the island, and it is also hunting for dinner.

From head to tail the fossa is four feet long, and it weighs more than 24 pounds. If given the chance, a fossa can kill an adult lemur. The red-brown animal is lanky but walks gracefully along the path. It uses the same trails we do and covers so much ground in one night's wanderings that it is seldom seen in the same place twice.

The fossa pauses and stares directly at me. This makes me nervous. Yet it doesn't seem that interested in me or bothered by the light from my headlamp.

Talata and I are captivated as we watch the hunter smell around the base of a tree. Its hind legs are noticeably taller than its front legs, so the animal's back arches above its low-set shoulders. The fossa rises up on its back legs, stretching up to test its retractable claws against the trunk's bark. These claws can move in or out of its paws just like the claws of a cat. I have read that fossas will eat almost anything, including birds, lizards, frogs, and rats. What does it smell up there?

With a push from its hind legs, the fossa begins to scale the tree, using its sharp claws to dig into the bark. Its muscular tail acts as a brace, providing balance and support. It rests on the first horizontal limb, then climbs higher. Now the fossa moves out onto a strong branch.

There's a large bird asleep on the same branch. It's a red-fronted coua, a common bird in the rain forest. The hunter creeps nearer, and the bird becomes alarmed. As it tries to spread its wings to fly, a large paw quickly slaps it down. The bird squawks and flutters but is soon held tightly by stout jaws.

The successful hunter descends the tree headfirst. Cautiously, with its prey dangling, the fossa moves into a sheltered spot. It starts to feed, and I can hear the cracking of bones.

It's been quite a night! We saw two species of carnivores. This hardly ever happens.

Back in my tent, I keep my headlamp on and write down everything I have seen, even making little drawings to show how the fossa climbed the tree. I need to remember all these details before they fade from my memory.

Only Worms

ANOTHER DAY OF RAIN. I WALK FOR HOURS AND SEE NO animal life. Then a glistening object on the trail catches my attention. There are giant earthworms here, almost two feet in length. When it rains for a long time, they crawl up from their holes to the surface. Spotting these huge worms as they stretch out and recoil to move over and under the decaying leaf litter, I jump several times, mistaking them for snakes.

Lemur Fight

THE RAIN CONTINUES TO FALL FOR SEVERAL DAYS. It's wonderful to be by the campfire: toasty warm on the front, but cold on the backside. I linger over a hot meal of rice topped with carrots and cabbage. With all the hiking I'm eating twice what I do at home, yet I'm still losing weight.

The long rains have brought out hundreds of thin, hungry leeches. They are everywhere in camp—on the forest floor, up in the trees, on my boots and in them. I watch a leech inch its way along, pausing to wave its mouth in the air.

The leech is trying to detect high levels of carbon dioxide, a gas given off by animals when they breathe. Because it is difficult for a leech to attach itself to fur, it is found most often on exposed skin. Some nights I take off my socks only to find them soaked with blood. Leeches crawl down into my socks and find my bare skin an easy target. If it's cold, I don't even feel the initial bite. The leech produces a substance that prevents blood from clotting. This allows a leech to drink freely from its host. Once full of blood, it drops off (or, in my case, gets caught in the toe of my sock), fat and well fed. Its body can swell to more than ten times its normal size. The leech will not need another meal for several months.

I finally pack up and head out into the forest at noon. If lemurs move in the rain, well, so can I. Today I am lucky. A family group of red-bellied lemurs is busy feeding on the fruit of a rahiaka (ra-HEE-ik-ka) tree just 30 yards from camp. This species of lemur, like the avahi, is monogamous, living in small family groups composed of an adult male and female with their young. The female reaches out and sniffs the rahiaka fruit, plucking off the ripest with her teeth. She bites into the fruit, eating the light green flesh and seeds. She consumes the fruit quickly, one after the other.

Her mate keeps watch. He is carrying their infant, who is only a few weeks old. Male red-bellied lemurs transport their infants most of the time, allowing the nursing mother to move freely in search of food. The youngster becomes playful and bobs around on its father's back. This is a good way to strengthen those little legs. The father is very attentive and reaches around to groom and lick the youngster.

After 20 minutes the female's hunger appears to be satisfied. She climbs down and gathers up the infant, who immediately starts to suckle. A few moments later a loud bark is heard. The female moves the baby onto her back and moves a short distance away. The male rises up on his hind legs, looking about. The two adults become increasingly nervous. A low *grrr* sound comes from the red-bellied lemurs.

A group of red-fronted lemurs has arrived in the nearby trees. Judging from the sound and the number of swaying tree branches that I see, it's a large group, perhaps eight to ten individuals. There may be a fight. Teeth grinding can be heard from both groups. A mock battle begins, each side uttering noisy threats at the other.

A red-fronted lemur makes a *cough-cough-wheeze* call as it crouches low on a tree branch, nervously looking around. The shy red-bellied lemurs are outnumbered and soon flee. The red-fronted lemurs are still excited and continue to scent mark the branches. They spread out into the foliage as they search for fruit, eating whatever they find, ripe or unripe.

As I watch the lemurs feed, I realize that the red-fronted and the red-bellied lemurs move differently from the other lemurs we have been watching. They don't keep their bodies vertical like the sifakas. They hold their bodies horizontal. The red-fronted and the red-bellied lemurs are quadrupeds: They walk on all four legs as a dog does.

A Tasty Snack

A YOUNG RED-FRONTED LEMUR CATCHES SIGHT OF a giant millipede more than four inches long crawling up a tree trunk. He grabs it just as the millipede recoils into a protective ball. What is he doing?

The lemur rolls the millipede back and forth between his hands. Soon he pulls his tail between his legs and rolls that together with the millipede. I'm glued to my binoculars and thinking, "Is he just playing?" The lemur glances over his shoulder at the others in his group and then pauses to taste the millipede. Judging from his reaction, it has a strong flavor, probably from the thick yellow ooze it's giving off. With a shake of his head, the red-fronted lemur begins to drool, and this is also rolled with the millipede. Then he gobbles it up.

I remember that this behavior was explained to me by another researcher who studies red-fronted lemurs. The lemur was "washing" the bad taste away.

The red-fronted lemurs spend several hours feeding on the small but crunchy fruit of the voapaka (vo-a-PACK-a) tree, along with leaves from several different species of climbing vines.

After the lemurs are full, they bed down for the night, huddling close together on the tree branches for warmth. They bury their heads into their bellies and pull their fluffy tails between their legs, up over their necks, and across their shoulders like a scarf. I stand up and stumble. My legs are cramped and half-asleep from sitting in one position for so long.

With so many fascinating things to observe, I forgot to have my lunch. I quickly eat a handful of roasted peanuts. I take a few bites of my cheese sandwich, then peek between my bread slices. No leeches, no millipedes!

Off to the Village

LIVING IN A CAMP IN THE MIDDLE OF A RAIN FOREST means walking out twice a month to buy food and other necessities. Today I'll be heading off to the nearest village. Talata will stay behind, as always, to guard the camp.

We eat Malagasy style, so I'll be bringing back lots of rice, beans, manioc (a long, starchy root), potatoes, and other assorted

vegetables. Perhaps I'll buy some fresh fruit and tomatoes, although they often get smashed in my pack before I arrive back in the forest. The sun beams overhead—it's a good, clear day for the three-hour hike.

Morning finds everyone in the village busy at their tasks. The pounding of rice echoes throughout the huts. Two women, each holding a large mortar, alternate in their movements as they pound the rice sheaf away from the grain. A few chickens cluster around the large wooden container, hunting for spilled rice.

The village huts look dry and comfortable, with their thick roofs made from bundles of dried grass. The framework is made from large bamboo poles. The walls are made of woven bamboo fibers.

A young boy races past a stone monument, a tribute to Madagascar's gaining independence from France in 1960. He guides a metal hoop with a stick as it rolls across the dirt-packed clearing and on down the slope toward the terraced rice fields.

The view is spectacular. The young rice shoots have been planted, and the landscape is a velvet carpet of green.

The streams that irrigate these rice fields originate in the mountains of the rain forest. The rain forest absorbs rainwater like a sponge. It traps moisture in the air and in the ground.

The villagers are fortunate that the Ranomafana forest is being preserved. Just a few hundred miles to the west, the forests have all been cut. Without the protective cover of plants, trees, and leaf litter, the soil is baked dry during the dry season. The rainy season causes massive landslides. The rootless earth erodes quickly, clogging the waterways with soil.

Good clean water and fertile soil are needed for planting and harvesting. Without them, farmlands turn into wastelands that are abandoned by the people who lived there.

Now that the Ranomafana forest is a national park, the trees can no longer be cut and burned to create new rice fields. All the rice for the village will have to come from the existing fields.

Nutrients must be put back into the soil so that rice can grow year after year. How will this be done? Will there be enough rice to sell or trade for needed clothes, machetes, and cooking utensils?

How will the people live?

One hope is to increase the rice yields. Malagasy specialists are working with experts from other countries to find ways to do this.

Villages can also benefit as researchers and tourists come to observe the unusual wildlife. These people need guides. Like Talata, many of the Malagasy grew up near the rain forest and know it well. Now they can share that knowledge and earn a salary doing work that will help preserve the riches of Ranomafana.

Yet, there are no quick answers. What if too many tourists come to the village? Some Malagasy worry that there won't be enough land for them to divide among their children. Will there be enough food for the grandchildren?

As human populations grow all over the world, the problem of dwindling agricultural land must be dealt with. Whatever the solution, the land must be healthy to support life. A healthy ecosystem is not just for animals. A healthy environment also means a healthy life for people.

I hike back into the forest with five porters. We carry the camp supplies in large duffel bags and in baskets on our heads. If only rice weren't so heavy and the village so far.

Lemur Chorus

WE ARE BACK IN THE FOREST, AND TODAY THE SKY IS A brilliant blue. Talata and I are hiking deep into the heart of the park. The trees spiral up to heights greater than 100 feet. Loud roaring calls split the air. Following this sound, we find a group of black-and-white ruffed lemurs.

There are several males and females sitting upright on the branches, exposing their bellies to the sun's warming rays. They look like little Buddhas. Black-and-white ruffed lemurs prefer to be up high in the trees and rarely venture down to the ground.

Their morning sunbath is interrupted by distant calls from another ruffed lemur group. A male immediately begins a low grunt that grows in pitch until it reaches an ear-shattering bark.

The others join in, the females adding a higher pitched bark, and the forest is alive with their chorus.

Then, as quickly as it began, it is over. This loud calling goes on throughout the day as each group lets the other groups know where it is.

Within seconds the ruffed lemurs are on the move, hurling their bodies between the gaps in the upper tree canopy with 20-foot leaps. They land in a spray of thin branches but quickly scamper along a larger tree limb and position themselves for the next jump. I run after them, watching as their black-and-white bodies move through the canopy.

It's a race I can't win. These lemurs tree hop while we struggle on foot through the thick underbrush. Several times I stumble over rocks and vines. Every field biologist worries about injuries because medical treatment is so far away. I slow down and choose my steps more carefully. Talata is faster. He stays with the lemurs while I try to catch up. He makes it possible for me to research lemur behavior.

The black-and-white ruffed lemurs grunt to one another as they work their way up the steep slope. I'm sweaty, exhausted, and my hands and arms sting from the scratches caused by prickly vines. The lemurs flush out a crested wood ibis. It is an enormous bird with a six-foot wingspan. I stop, amazed at its ability to navigate in such dense foliage. The ibis's wing tips hit several branches until it rises above the canopy and flies off with its long orange legs trailing behind.

We continue to follow the ruffed lemurs as long as we can, but eventually they outdistance us.

Encounter with a Grub Specialist

AFTER SLEEPING MOST OF THE DAY IN PREPARATION FOR a long night of lemur searching, I spend time looking up information in the bird and mammal guidebooks that I keep in my tent. These help me with basic information about what lemurs eat, where they sleep, and where they live on the island. This background work helps me understand the behaviors I observe. At the same time, there is so much we still don't know about these animals.

I've been here for four months and there are lemurs I still haven't seen: the fat-tailed dwarf lemur, the sportive lemur, the golden bamboo lemur, and the aye-aye.

Some days ago, Talata spotted an aye-aye's nest. With his help, I may see this creature tonight.

Before heading out, we eat a big meal of rice and beans. Wispy clouds pass overhead, and the moon is almost full. It's an excellent night for tracking. We split an after-dinner chocolate bar for added stamina and to boost our morale.

Unexpectedly, two broad-striped mongooses appear out of the darkness, scouting our cook area. Undoubtedly they are a male and female pair. I read in my guidebook that for their size they have massive canines, the large, pointed teeth characteristic of carnivores. They are strictly meat eaters.

The pair investigates a snare of fallen logs, gliding in and out of the brambles with their whiskers quivering. They pause for a few seconds in a graceful stance. The male and female of this species are inseparable. When one is out of sight, it uses a whistle-like call to let the other know its whereabouts.

After inspecting a spot near an old rat den, the fur bristles on the mongooses' tails, showing their excitement. But the two prowlers are jittery. Before I can get my camera, they're gone.

As we continue through the night forest, it feels alive. We're surrounded by the blinking glow of fireflies. Geckos and tree frogs serenade us with their croaks and grunts.

We arrive at the nest just in time to hear a rustle overhead. In the beams from our headlamps and flashlights, we watch a head emerge from the large, leafy nest about 12 feet above the ground. The animal's sensitive ears tremble and twitch in response to the noises of the night.

The aye-aye pulls its head back inside the nest but reappears a few seconds later and moves out onto the branch. It licks its hands, paying careful attention to its long, tapered fingers, especially the bony middle finger.

The aye-aye's mouth is small, yet two large incisors slightly protrude, which makes the mouth look like it is always a bit open.

The aye-aye reaches behind, grooming its back and working down to its large, foxlike tail. Abruptly the animal freezes, as a bird screeches in the distance. The lemur looks at us in a curious fashion, then moves down the tree and follows a fallen branch to the ground.

With its pushed-in face and short, muscular neck, the aye-aye is an unusual-looking animal. It may not be as attractive as other lemur species, but I remind myself that, pretty or not, it deserves as much respect and protection as the others. Besides, aye-ayes must find other aye-ayes attractive!

The aye-aye straddles a dead log. Its long, bushy tail arches out behind as its nose presses to the wood, sniffing for food. The lemur focuses on a likely spot and begins a series of fast but gentle taps. Its batlike ears rotate forward and down around its tapping finger, perhaps to shut out background noise. A low, dull sound follows a hollow-sounding tap: Wood-boring grubs may be in the passageways just below the bark. The aye-aye wedges its incisors into the bark and uses them like a crowbar to pry the bark away. Large chips of wood fly into the air. Several soft white grubs are soon exposed and quickly eaten.

The aye-aye then uses its long, clawed, middle finger to probe for more insects. The finger moves as if it is made of rubber rather than bone, negotiating the maze of tunnels.

Talata whispers that some Malagasy eat the white grubs found in rotting palm trees. They are roasted over the fire and taste just like butter. I look at him and smile, thinking he is teasing me. He assures me it's true.

The aye-aye pulls its finger out of the log. A fat grub is skewered on its claw. The lemur pauses, puts the grub into its mouth, and looks about while its jaws work to mash up the fat larva. Then, without warning, the aye-aye is done. It begins to climb a tree. I have no idea why it's left the log. Have all the grubs been fished out? Or, perhaps it wants something different to eat.

Soon we lose sight of the lemur in the thick canopy as a soft rain shower begins. Rain makes it nearly impossible to see or hear anything at night.

From the work of other field biologists, we know that to sustain its six-pound body, the aye-aye consumes nutritious beetle larvae, plant and insect galls, and fruit seeds. Because the Ranomafana forest is an old forest littered with dead and dying trees full of grubs, it provides prime habitat for one of the world's rarest primates.

The Golden Bamboo Lemur

WE'VE BEEN OUT WALKING ALL NIGHT. AS I STARE INTO the foliage, my tired eyes begin to see funny shapes. The shadows cast by my headlamp confuse me. I think I see eyeshine, but no, it's just beads of rainwater reflecting back at me. I'm tired. It's been a great night, but now it's time to go home.

Dawn breaks as Talata and I near camp. All I want to do is crawl onto my lumpy cot and sleep. But the forest never sleeps. Now that the nocturnal animals have retired, others have awakened.

I gaze up at a blue coua sunning itself in the uppermost branches of a tall rotra (ROO-tra) tree. It puffs up its feathers, its tail fully flared as it shakes itself, scattering water droplets. The coua settles down again and, with its bill open, sends out a series of descending *coy, coy, coy, coy, coy, coy* calls.

I pretend the bird is saying "good morning" to Talata and me.

Nearby, a small lemur shakes its wet fur, peers around, and climbs down from a dense tangle of bamboo stems. It's a male golden bamboo lemur! His head is roundish with small cub ears. A mantle of gold fur surrounds his face and trickles down onto his chest and belly. The rest of his body is dark brown. The lemur appears to be hungry. Immediately he bites off a piece of bamboo several feet long.

He then strips off the tough outer layer and feasts on the inner core. There are three species of lemurs in Ranomafana who like this food; all have the word "bamboo" in their names.

Seeing the golden bamboo lemur is so unexpected. Now his mate appears and descends from her hidden sleep spot. She grabs the tip of a large bamboo shoot, strips off the tough outer sheaths, and eats the soft, white interior. Like the avahi, this lemur species is monogamous.

Both animals continue to satisfy their appetites, munching and crunching bamboo. The golden bamboo lemur is unusual, because it can feed on parts of the giant bamboo that are laced with cyanide. In a single day, a three-pound golden bamboo lemur consumes 12 times the lethal dose of cyanide for an animal its size. It even prefers bamboo shoots, the part of the plant where the poison is concentrated. No other primate is known to tolerate such high levels of poison.

The golden bamboo lemur was first discovered in 1986 by scientists in this rain forest. It's incredibly rare to find a scientifically unknown species of primate now that so much of the world has been explored. This discovery was one of the many reasons the Ranomafana forest was established as a protected area.

Golden bamboo lemurs are among the treasures to be found in Ranomafana National Park. Who knows what other secrets its mountain ridges and secluded valleys may hold?

*Readers interested in finding out more about
Ranomafana National Park may write to the following address:*

Institute for the Conservation of Tropical Environments (ICTE)

*SUNY at Stony Brook
SBS Building, 5th Floor
Stony Brook, New York 11794-4364*